CALVIN MILLER

BUCKETS OF NOTHING

The Story of Creation in Rhyme

Illustrated by
Marc Harrison

THOMAS NELSON PUBLISHERS
Nashville • Camden • Kansas City

Published in Nashville, Tennessee, by Thomas Nelson,
Inc. and distributed in Canada by Lawson Falle, Ltd.,
Cambridge, Ontario.
Printed in the United States of America.
ISBN 0-8407-6719-6   1 2 3 4 5 — 91 90 89 88 87

Have you ever wondered
Why God made this earth
With its beavers and babies
And bunnies and birds?

And beetles and bulldogs,
And bogs that abound
With black spotted frogs
Making croak-awful sounds?

There's something to see
Wherever you gaze.
God made all the world,
And aren't you amazed
That God made it all
In only six days?

Now before God made anything
Nothing was here.
Nothing was far.
And nothing was near.

Nothing was ground,
And nothing was air.
There was plenty of nothing—
Just everywhere!

Wherever there's nothing
You'll always find black.
In nothing there always
Is plenty of that.

I can't say how much
But there was no lack,
Maybe ten million, sextillion
Buckets of black!

But one day God said,
"This black makes me lonely.
Who needs all this black?
It's like walking around
With my head in a sack.
Ten million, sextillion
Buckets of night is
Much too much nothing.
So let there be light!"

Wow!

The black all turned white,
Ten million, sextillion
Buckets of light!
There still was some black,
But it drew back in fright.
It shivered and shook,
Afraid of the light.

Till God said out loud,
"This scaredy-cat black,
I think I'll call night."
God knew there were times
When we don't need much light,
Like when we're asleep,
Then lonely's all right.
And black when we're sleeping
Just isn't a fright.

The second day came and
God said, "Well, I'll be!
Now that there's light
I'd like something to see.
Who could be lonely
With something to see?
I'll start making something.
Now what will it be?"

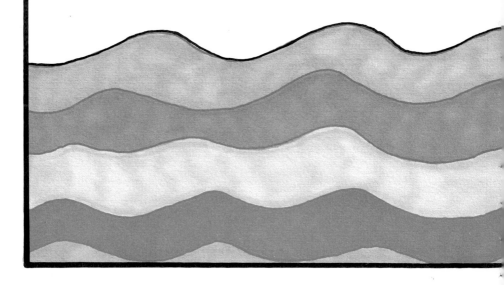

"I think I'll make water.
I'll need lots of water
When I make the sea.
Hey, water! C'mon,
You can start running free."
So water came running
And sloshing and dashing
And dripping and flashing,
And spilling and pouring,
And flooding and splashing.

The third day God just
Couldn't help grinning.
"This water's O.K.
If you only go swimming.
But I want to walk
On firm, solid ground.
I've made so much water,
There's no ground around.

"So I think it's time
That I wave my hand.
And each time I wave it
I'll make lots of land."
God waved, there was land—
Just as He had planned.

As God spoke again
His voice shook the air.
"This land looks too bare,
And bare land is lonely.
I'll plant something there.
Hey! Grass!
You can sprout now—
Just sprout everywhere!"

And little green blades
Sprouted. Sproing! Sproing!
And the trees shot up, too.
Kerboing and kerboing!

That very same day
God also made weeds
And big dandelions
With parachute seeds.

And then on the fourth day,
God said, "Things are gray!
I think I'll make something
Too fiery to hide.
Something to make me
Feel sunny inside."
So God started working,
And when He was done,
He made a big fireball
And called it the sun.

The fifth day was great.
God stayed up quite late
Making fishes and tadpoles,
And porpoises and whales.
And cobras and eels,
And slick, slimy snails.

And birds, owls, and eagles,
And parrots and scagulls.

Day six came at last,
And God finished His task.
He made all the wart hogs
And long-necked giraffes!
When God saw how long
Their necks were, He laughed,
"I've made these giraffes
Just as I should.
There are times
When a seven-foot neck
Is quite good.

"They'll love to eat leaves
From the top of the trees.
They'll need those long necks
And those long, bony knees.
They're gracefully tall,
All spotted and specky.
It's good I have made
Them so leggy and necky."

Even after giraffes
God was lonely, it's true,
So He made seven hundred
And seventy-two
More marvelous things,
Like chipmunks and shrews.

And just before lunch
God looked at the crowd
Of things He had made
And then said out loud,
"I think I'll make
A huge gray machine
With a tail on each end
And a hulk in between.
This oversized beastie
Will not be a runt.
He'll be six thousand pounds
Of trumpet and grunt.

I think I will call him
A gray elephant!"

"I'm lonely," God said.
"I wish elephants
Could do something more than
Just trumpet and grunt.
They're big and they're nice,
But they've nothing to say.
They just stand around
Eating peanuts all day.

"I'm still very lonely.
I know what I'll do.
I'll make me a man
Who is just six-foot-two,
Who can go for a walk
And talk now and then,
So I will not ever
Be lonely again."

And God did just that.
In one wink of His eye,
Adam was made.
He stood and said, "My!
It's so good to be here,
Just look at that sky!"

God smiled!
"For millions of years,
Adam, millions on end,
I've been lonely—so lonely
Will you be my friend?"

"Forever," laughed Adam,
"I need a friend, too."

And this is why God
Made both me and you.

Will God ever quit
Being friends with us?
Never!
God's friendship is special.
His friends are forever!